Fly Free!

An Australian Birds Hide and Seek

The outback of Australia is big and wide
There are so many places for you to hide
With colorful birds of varying kinds
Let's take a peek and see what we find

The Sulphur-crested Cockatoo sits tall and free
He makes his nest in big hollow trees
You might see him standing on the ground
Sometimes that's where his next meal is found

The Zebra Finch might look very small
But don't let his size fool you at all!
These cute clever birds don't make a peep
Their typical sounds are more like a beep!

In the grassland, Parakeets can be seen
Their tails are long and feathers are green
Parakeets have ceres to tell who is who
Females have brown while males have blue.

Cockatiels like to whistle all day through
You can see them in different colors too
To learn their mood, watch their crest on top
Up means they're happy, down means stop!

Eclectus parrots are all very smart
They love eating fruits just for a start
Females are bright red and males are green
That makes them much easier to be seen!

Lorikeets look like rainbows in flight
With colorful bodies, what a beautiful sight!
They like to drink nectar and think it's great fun
Doing this is easy with their brush-like tongue.

Rosella's are lovely and come in bright red
They chatter all day until time for bed
They live in the forest and in trees so high
If you're lucky enough, you'll see one in the sky

King-Parrots lay eggs in the trunk of a tree
Their typical clutch is five eggs, you see
The difference between them can easily be seen
Males have red heads and females have green.

The Galah's colors are pink, gray and white
They are easy to spot while they're in flight
They gather in a flock to eat off the ground
Hundreds of birds, oh, what a sound!

Kookaburras sit up tall and proud
Their laughing call is extremely loud!
They like to eat animals, like mice and snakes
And find them tastier than chocolate cakes!

The Great Albatross is last but not least
His wingspan can get to over twelve feet!
He lives near the water and fishes all day
If you are lucky, you might see him near a bay.

The Australian Outback is home to them all
In every season, even the fall
These birds fly free and like it that way
Remember that, if you see one someday.

Publisher's Cataloging- In-Publication Data

Bartlett, Katherine

Fly Free! An Australian Birds Hide and Seek / by Katherine Bartlett ;
Illustrated by Mary P. Biswas

p. : col. ill. ; cm.

Summary: The Australian Outback is a large and mysterious place. It is home to many different types of birds. Can you find the parrots hiding on each page?

Interest Age Level: 4-8.
Interest Grade Level: P-3.

ISBN 13: 978-0692914557
ISBN 10: 0692914552

1. Birds--Juvenile literature. 2. Picture puzzles--Juvenile literature. 3. Australia--Juvenile literature. 4. Stories in rhyme.5. Birds. 6. Picture puzzles.

Animal Tales Press
Atlanta, GA

About the Author

Katherine Bartlett has been in love with birds for as long as she can remember. When she was a child, she grew up in a house full of dogs and cats so when she finally got old enough, she got her first two parakeets, Pete and Belle. Soon after that, her bird family grew quickly!

Currently she has seven American Parakeets, 1 Zebra Finch, 2 Cockatiels, 1 Lovebird, 1 Pineapple Conure, 1 Parrolet and 1 Pekin Duck. And of course she hopes to have more birds one day!

Katherine resides in the Southeast with her husband and seven year old daughter.